C000021231

BEADLE'S ABOUT

**A BEHIND THE SCENES LOOK
AT LWT'S HIT SERIES**

YOU

COULD BE
A POTENTIAL STAR OF
BEADLE'S ABOUT

Yes, you!

BEADLE'S ABOUT

WHO'S WHO ON BEADLE'S ABOUT

Producer Robert Randell
Directors Sue McMahon, Chris Fox
Designer Bob Day
Associate Producer Alan Hopkins
Programme Associate Ian Cross
Researchers Ann Cornell
Rob Clark
Louise Stellakis
Joanna Stewart
Production Assistant Nicky Bryant
Stage Manager Stephen Joel
Programme Manager Katy Bearman
Location Manager Simon Wallace

First published in Great Britain in 1989
by Sidgwick and Jackson Limited

Copyright © 1989 by London Weekend Television

Written by Robert Randell

Designed by Hammond Hammond

Illustrations by Chris Lloyd

Project co-ordinator: Alan Hopkins
Picture researcher: Helen Thickling

Produced by Grub Street

ISBN 0–283–99936–5

Photoset by Chapterhouse, Formby L37 3PX

Printed in Great Britain by Eagle Press
for Sidgwick & Jackson Limited
1 Tavistock Chambers, Bloomsbury Way
London WC1A 2SG

I'M A VERY LUCKY MAN. I work with some of the most talented people in television – my production team – and I get to meet some of the nicest people in the country – you, the public.

On average, we receive about 10,000 letters a year from members of the public wanting to play a joke on loved ones, friends or colleagues. This book tells you how we fashion this raw material into one of the most popular and innovative shows on British television. Indeed, we are so successful our ideas and techniques are copied around the world!

A number of people have been critical to the success of the programme but I owe a particular debt to the following:

Alan Boyd, who as Controller of Entertainment at LWT gave me my break on *Game For A Laugh* and later commissioned *Beadle's About*

Marcus Plantin, the current Controller, who not only kept faith with the programme but has also encouraged me to develop in other areas

Robert Randell, my producer and friend, whose deep understanding of television and comedy turned *Beadle's About* into the huge hit it is

My family, Leo, Clare, Cassie, Bunnie, Mary and Harry for their support and love

And Sue, who makes every day smile.

That sort of back-up has made making *Beadle's About* an immense pleasure.

Like I said, I'm a lucky man!

Jeremy Beadle

THE YEAR-LONG PRODUCTION DIARY

January — Read letters/discuss story lines with Producer.

N.B. Try to organize a weekend away.

February — Read more letters/discuss story lines with associate producer and researchers.

N.B. Try to organize a weekend away.

March — Set up filming.

N.B. MUST organize a weekend away.

April
May
June
July
August — Filming and first studios.

N.B. Defer weekend away till Autumn

September
October — Filming and studios.

N.B Forget weekend away. Try to organize AUTUMN holiday

November — Edit programmes.

N.B. Try to book WINTER holiday

December — FREE AT LAST!

N.B. All winter and 'SUN' holidays are fully booked.

January — Read letters/discuss story lines with Producer.

N.B. Try to organize a weekend away!

A GLOSSARY OF TERMS USED BY THE *BEADLE'S ABOUT* GANG – OR BEADLESPEAK

PLEASE READ THIS.

OTHERWISE YOU WILL NOT UNDERSTAND THE REST OF THE BOOK!

PUNTER A term of affection used to describe any person who is the victim of a *Beadle's About* wheeze

QUICKIE A simple practical joke played on unsuspecting passers-by in the street

SET-UP A much more elaborate joke than a 'quickie'; 'set-ups' always involve the 'punter' being set-up by his or her family, friends or colleagues

SCAM Originally, an American expression meaning a confidence trick, loosely applied to a *Beadle's About* set-up

WIND-UP The basic joke being played upon a punter

HIT The actual process of playing the joke

TO 'BUY' To 'buy' a wind-up is to be taken in by the joke

HAVING 'BOUGHT' Having 'bought' a wind-up means to have been taken in by the joke

TO 'BLOW' To lose one's temper. Thus punters usually 'blow' when 'wound up'

TO SUSS To 'suss' something is to see that a joke is about to played or is being played. Thus a punter *might* 'suss the wind-up'

TAG A comic twist at the end of a set-up

THE 'REVEAL' The 'reveal' occurs when Jeremy removes his disguise or produces his stick microphone. At this point the punter will certainly 'suss the wind-up'

GONE BANANAS Seized by an uncontrollable fit of laughter. A temporary state of extreme anger or mental instability induced in a punter when he or she has really 'bought the wind-up' and is complaining bitterly about, say, the forty pigs in the garden. Thus, 'The punter has bought the wind-up and is going bananas'

WOOFER An anticipated level of laughter from the studio or home audience. Thus, 'It'll get woofers when they see the punter going bananas'

BELTER An anticipated level of laughter from the studio or home audience at a higher level than a woofer. Thus; 'Funny? It'll get you belters!'

SCREAMER An anticipated level of laughter from the studio or home audience at a higher volume than a belter. The highest possible laugh level. Much sought after by entertainment producers

TO CORPSE For an actor (including Jeremy!) to start laughing in the middle of the scam

MONEY IN THE BANK A rock solid success

BIG RED NOSE, WHIRLY BOW-TIE TELEVISION The producer's way of explaining how *Beadle's About* differs from *Panorama*, *Horizon* and *Songs of Praise*, etc

FROCKS Any item of costume worn by an actor or actress. Thus, 'What sort of frock shall we get for Francis Gainsborough in the swimming pool scam?

SLAP Any kind of make-up, excluding wigs and beards, etc

Now translate the following:

THAT PUNTER WENT BANANAS WHEN WE HIT HIM WITH THE WIND-UP. AND WHEN HE SUSSED IT ON THE REVEAL IT WAS SCREAMERS ALL THE WAY. WHAT A SCAM! MONEY IN THE BANK!

WHERE IT ALL STARTS

While the series is being transmitted, the *next* series is taking shape. Thousands of letters begin to clog the postroom at LWT. Throughout November and December the producer reads and assesses *every single letter*. There are also sorted into cities and counties. From approximately ten thousand letters a 'long list' of about four hundred letters is prepared. They are stored in lever arch files along with an index.

If these files are lost there is no series – it's as simple as that.

These files *never* leave the office.

LETTERS

Thousands upon thousands of letters are sent to *Beadle's About*. What makes a letter worth following up?

A LETTER GUARANTEED TO BE FOLLOWED UP

punter is very excitable

112 Primrose Lane
Landcaster
Loamshire

Dear Jeremy,

If you want to see somebody really go mad you ought to see my dad when the Gas Board dug up his lawn five times in six months. He says that if they come again there will be murder.

Do you think you could think of something to get him going? You can phone me on my work telephone number 0243-68261.

Yours sincerely,

Louise Parsons

NO PROBLEM

there's a story we can exploit!

letter writer can be contacted secretly

Typed letters are so much easier to read and therefore to assess and people who type letters usually take the trouble to include all the relevant information, too!

Nothing to go on at all

112 Primrose Lane
Landcaster,
Loamshire

Dear Jeremy,
My Dad is always playing jokes on me. Can you think of a joke to play on him? Please.
Love, Louise.

Louise WHO!   How contacted?

Not such a good letter

A PERSON TO BE AVOIDED

Why? read on

112 Primrose Lane
Landcaster
Loanshire

Dear Jeremy,
I have worked out a smashing joke to play on Mark Williams. Mark is twenty-four and is the proud possessor of an X-reg. Ford Cortina GHIA. It is his pride and joy. He absolutely lives for his car.

Now, here's the joke. You see, every Sunday Mark drives to his local for a game of darts and a drink with his pals. And he always parks in the same place – near an old wall that is beginning to crumble. My idea is to collapse the wall on Mark's car!

So far so good, but see how it ends.

I can tell you Mark will go completely bonkers and it would be very funny. By the way, if you play the joke on Mark please don't tell him that it was my idea because we broke off our engagement two weeks ago. My work telephone number is 0243-68261.

Yours sincerely,

Louise Parsons

HEAVEN HATH NO RAGE LIKE LOVE TO HATE TURN'D

HELL HATH NO FURY LIKE A WOMAN SPURN'D

AND FINALLY: CAN *YOU* READ IT?

JEREMY BEADLE SPELLING DISASTERS

O ver the course of the four *Beadle's About* series tens of thousands of letters have been received in the production office. Below are lists of the various spellings of the two seemingly simple names.

GERMY (!?!)	BEGALL
JERRERMY	BEEGLE
JERMMY	BEEGAL
JERMY	BEEGEL
JERMAMY	BIGGLE
JERERMEE	BIGLE
JERERMY	BEEDLE
(getting close)	(getting close)

BRIEFEST ADDRESSED ENVELOPE EVER RECEIVED

BEAGLE TELEVISION

was put on the envelope   no stamps either!

WHAT HAPPENS TO THE LETTERS THAT DON'T GO FORWARD TO SHORT LISTING?

F ew letters are thrown away. Nearly every letter is filed under town or county. Even a seemingly unpromising letter of the 'Could you think of a joke to play on my wife?' type could be of eventual use. Frequently, the team will think of an idea then have to find the punters to fit the situation! That's when the researchers start trawling the files for possible leads.

THE PEOPLE WHO WRITE INTO BEADLE

W ithout the people who write in there would not be a series of *Beadle's About*. So here's a selection of those responsible for some of your favourite scams.

'Political Billboard'

Margaret Ford   **SET UP**   Linda Bidgood

'Swimming Pool'

Donna Hambidge   **SET UP**   Bert Hambidge

'Drag Act'

Steve Wilson   **SET UP**   Sue Wilson

'Frascati'

Gaynor Round   **SET UP**   Tony Moroncini

THE FIRST DISCUSSIONS

During the last two weeks of January, Jeremy and the producer discuss each idea on the long list. Their basic litmus test is: 'If we fall about laughing at an idea, then the viewers will.' Most of the time they are rolling about the floor laughing. But when they are not killing themselves laughing, each idea is discussed in great detail and a basic 'story line' agreed. It's an almost telepathic relationship because they seldom disagree. But they do have one rule: if Jeremy, for any reason, really hates the idea it doesn't go ahead. Or, if the producer really hates an idea it doesn't go ahead. The system is simple. And it works. There is *never* argument.

The long list of four hundred letter-based ideas is pared down to a short list of about one hundred. This list is typed, printed and will be distributed to the production team.

HOW A LETTER TURNS INTO A STORYLINE

During these early discussions the producer flicks through the letters in the lever arch files.

'The next letter is from a Vivienne Apps from West Malling in Kent,' informs the producer. 'She wants to play a joke on her father.'

'Any history?' enquires Jeremy.

'Yes,' replies the producer, 'Get a load of this: thirty years ago the council took the top third of his garden to build a warden's house for a nearby park. Since then he's turned the garden into something out of Kew Gardens and he's terrified that the council are going to come along again.'

Jeremy begins to chuckle – the comic possibilities are coming thick and fast.

'Well,' continues the producer, 'couldn't we turn his garden into a council tea garden and his garage into public loos?'

But Jeremy simply gazes into the far distance. 'Love the idea about hijacking his garage for loos, but can't we really turn his little bit of Eden into a nightmare?'

'Mmmm,' muses the producer, 'what about some sort of sewage plant, perhaps?'

Jeremy doesn't respond; he's still in a world of his own. 'What about a garden gnome sanctuary?' he enquires, quietly.

The producer practically slips off his chair laughing. 'Why don't we make it a museum of garden gnomes?' he blurts before collapsing into uncontrollable laughter. By this time Jeremy has 'gone' too.

When both sober up somewhat the rest of the basic story line is bolted into place: an insensitive 'council' official to tell our punter that his garden is being annexed in the interests of 'culture'; a stroppy 'council' worker who will be responsible for converting the garage into loos and a rather silly, over-effusive representative from the 'Gnome Appreciation Society'. Convulsed with laughter, neither can even think about what role Jeremy will play or what sort of comedy 'tag' will end the scam. But Jeremy is ultimately cast as 'Uncle Percy' – a full-sized gnome from Devon who will be used for publicity purposes. And the tag? The punter will be expected to dress up in a similar costume to fulfil his roll as the unpaid warden of the Gnome Museum!

From one letter a basic story line has emerged within minutes.

A GNOME'S NIGHTMARE

THE GANG GET TOGETHER

B y the middle of March the series production team is 'up and running' and preparing for the first day's filming.

WHAT DO ALL THESE PEOPLE DO?

He says he's so busy on the show he doesn't have time for a love life!

including his HAIR·DO.

THE PRODUCER

Basically, he selects the scams for the series and makes sure that they happen on time and within the budget. The buck stops on his desk.

WHO'S HE TRYING TO KID!

THE DIRECTORS

The film directors have one very basic but very difficult job: to get the shots. It is absolutely vital that the directors get close-ups of the punters *at all times* – defocussed backs of heads do not get woofers!

THE DESIGNER

Apart from designing the studio set the designer is totally responsible for making any scam *look* absolutely believable – a travel agents' office *must* be authentic.

THE ASSOCIATE PRODUCER

The associate producer is responsible for co-ordinating the research effort. When an 'angle' has been decided with the researcher and the producer the 'AP' will liaise with the programme associate to develop the story.

THE PROGRAMME ASSOCIATE

The programme associate's job is to dream up funny angles and to collate the funny angles generated by everybody else on the team in the form of the script. It takes great skill and diplomacy to blend everybody's two pennyworth to the satisfaction of the producer!

THE RESEARCHERS

The researchers are the core part of the operation: basically, they must unearth or develop a plausible story line for each scam and then make it happen. *Then take the BLAME*

THE PRODUCTION ASSISTANT

The production assistant should really be called the 'production co-ordinator.' She is not involved in everything but she knows all about everything! A good P.A. should be naturally nosy!

Including the skeletons in everybody's cupboards

actually his letter booking them that!

THE STAGE MANAGER

The stage manager is directly responsible for the liaison between the production team and the service departments. If you want a pink elephant with mauve spotted ears then the 'Ess-Em' is your man!

THE PROGRAMME MANAGER

The programme manager is responsible for keeping a very accurate track of every penny being spent on the series. Not an altogether popular figure when she suggested that the entire team travel everywhere by bike!

THE LOCATION MANAGER

The location manager will organize all travel, accommodation and catering arrangements for the day's filming – and also all 'permissions' – police, nearby residents, etc. A much respected figure, if he can make a habit of organizing cooked breakfasts!

Everything is always HIS FAULT!

FIRST DECISIONS

Basic 'on-the-telephone' research has yielded some very promising stories. What happens next? Simple – what is called 'legwork'. This is basic research, and without it the series wouldn't happen. The researchers make secret calls, say, to the wife who wants to set up her husband. The 'location' is secretly visited and the basic 'plot' is discussed with whoever is doing the setting up. Exhaustive checks are made to find out whether a suggested punter is, in fact, suitable to be 'Beadled'.

Is this a Verb, Noun or just a swear word?

WE GO AHEAD

When the researcher returns from, say, covertly watching a prospective punter play a game of darts in his local, six questions have got to be answered to the satisfaction of the associate producer.

1. Is there any medical reason why we should not 'Beadle' this punter? Has the medical history been thoroughly checked?

2. Is it possible to hide the cameras on the location?

3. Is the basic story plausible?

4. Will our punter 'buy the wind-up'?

5. Will our punter see the joke afterwards? and, of course . . .

6. Will our punter recognize Jeremy when we do the reveal?

If we get 'yes' six times then it is full steam ahead. With the AP, the researcher will begin to dig out real 'history' that can be woven into the scam. For example, we might obtain any correspondence our punter has written to the council and forge replies that he never received.

If the basic story isn't plausible given the punter's background, then it might be possible to change tack. If we can't dig up his lawn, how about turning his garage into a council gritting depot? What is vital is that any situation developed is plausible enough for the punter to 'buy it'.

Very rarely, a story will fall down completely. The location may be impossible to film in, the story might be too weak or the punter might be distressed by any sort of wind-up. So work starts on another story.

THE OTHER IDEAS

WHAT ABOUT A FAT MAN AND AN ARAB WITH A CAMEL?

NO – A THIN MAN, AN IRISHMAN AND AN ARMADILLO! SURELY?

A very rare photo of a 'discreet' researcher equipped to undertake covert surveillance of a punter!

But *Beadle's About* doesn't just rely on situations sent in by viewers. The 'comedy sketch' ideas are generated by Jeremy, the producer and the entire production team. Somebody will say, 'Wouldn't it be a laugh if we would get some bloke to do a drag act in front of his wife at a night club?' The tag being that she wouldn't realize it was him until the reveal. Everybody then crashes in with ideas and within seconds a basic scenario has been formed. That's how 'Drag Act' came into existence. Sometimes, a researcher will stumble upon an idea that nobody has ever thought of. Or, rather, a unique idea will simply collide with the researcher.

The important thing is that the production team members aren't 'precious'. They do not really worry who originates the idea so long as it is funny. And, crucially, everybody on the team has the chance to make a decisive creative contribution to the programme. That's the joy of doing the show. All the comedy sketch ideas are typed and printed to form a companion volume to the letters list.

HOW THE GOLIGHTLY FAMILY WAS BORN

Jeremy and the producer were having a meal after an ideas session. Jeremy ventured the opinion that he ought to lose a bit of weight. The producer mused: 'Do you know, I really would like to see a titanically fat man go into a furniture shop and collapse all the furniture.'

Picking up the picture, Jeremy replied: 'It would be funnier if it could be a bed shop – and we weakened all the beds, too!' Convulsed with mirth, a forkful of lasagne nearly propelled itself from the producer's mouth. But they were almost there. Asked the producer: 'Why don't we play the joke on a "temporary manager" sent along specially?' 'Could do,' said Jeremy, 'but why don't we make it a family of fat people who crush the beds – one by one?' Both cracked up at this point but the now famous Golightly family was born.

The programme associate fleshed out a script involving Jeremy as a 'Mr Derek Walker' who would turn up to collect the smashed beds. Researcher Anne Cornell found a bed shop and organized the arrival of the 'temporary manager'. The specially wrecked beds were installed, and the cameras were hidden. An actor was cast to play the part of the manager who would leave our temps in charge of the shop. The scene was set. Disaster piled upon disaster and a classic was born.

Or at least distribute more evenly what I've already got!

just around the corner from where she lives. She calls it DEEP RESEARCH!

A WEIGHTY PROBLEM

HOW 'DRAG ACT' HAPPENED

It was about 6.30 one spring evening. The producer had his feet up and was gazing at a particularly attractive sunset from the fifteenth floor of Kent House. Alan Hopkins, then a researcher, ambled across to the producer's desk. 'I've been thinking,' mused Alan. 'We haven't done a secret skill for ages – since the first series, in fact.'

And he was SOBER!

'Mmmm,' replied the producer, 'but they did most of them on *Game for a Laugh*; and we did the best one when we got the masked bloke to do an exotic dance in front of his wife. Where do we go next? We can't have a woman doing a strip when her husband goes to some stag do, can we?'

'Well', ventured Alan, 'I wonder if we could get some woman along to a hen night and get her husband to do a drag act before we reveal him to her?'

The producer sat upright, the aesthetics of the sunset forgotten. 'I buy that!' he exclaimed.

He did - but never paid for it.

The programme associate rapidly cottoned onto the possibilities. 'He could do a whole act!' he breathed in wonderment. From that simple beginning flowered one of the most organizationally complex scams ever to be attempted by the *Beadle's About* team.

Within hours a complete scenario had been developed. The drag act would be called 'Fräulein Marlene' – the German character giving the means by which the punter's voice could be disguised. After an introduc-

A SURPRISE IN DISGUISE

tory song to 'set the mood' our 'Fräulein Marlene' would do a mentalist act. And, of course, our 'Fräulein Marlene' would pick on the wife to participate in the act! The 'Fräulein' would know *all* the wife's details! But getting that close to the wife could cause our husband to be recognized – even in drag! So the decision was made to conceal half the face with a 'diadem' mask.

Secret training

At this point, the team had a great idea and a workable scenario. But next came the difficult bit – finding a *suitable* husband/wife combination *and* secretly training him to become a drag act capable of performing in front of some two hundred raucous women at a hen night. A fairly tall order!

Alan's first initiative was to check all the files to find a man who wanted to play a joke upon his wife. A number of possibilities were explored but all led to a dead end. Alan was getting worried: great story, no star! Eventually, he contacted a punter from a previous scam who enjoyed a wide range of friends and contacts. And, yes, he could suggest a possible contact for the idea. Alan chased up the name and telephone number and found himself the perfect candidate for this very difficult scam – Steve Wilson, a thirty-seven-year-old power worker from Essex, married to Sue for eleven years, with

two small children. Upon meeting Steve it was obvious that he would not have any hang-ups about training as a drag artiste. An important point. But this was not as easy as it sounds because Steve had to be trained secretly. On no account must his wife find out. By arranging to take the odd afternoon off work and by telling flagrant lies to his wife ('off for a round of golf, dear' etc.) Steve

A big word meaning easily led and willing.

The performance side of the whole thing was only 50 per cent of the problem. It was necessary to find a pub or club to stage a hen night featuring Fräulein Marlene and to find a pretext for getting Sue along.

Uproar

On the basis that nothing is impossible, Alan set up and co-ordinated an entire hen night in a pub in Kent together with a complete range of acts to add to the authenticity. It was arranged for a somewhat reluct-ant Sue to come along to the hen night on the pretext that it was a treat organized by the 'friend of a friend'. One key problem remained: it was necessary to convince Sue that Steve would stay at home to babysit whilst she enjoyed her night out with the girls. Sue waved goodbye not knowing that minutes later Steve would be in a fast car heading for Kent while Sue took a rather roundabout route! While Sue was travelling Steve was shaving his legs, plucking his eyebrows, putting on his make-up and wig before wriggling into the specially upholstered dress.

In spite of never having performed before, Steve was brilliant. Sue bought it completely and had no idea that the strange German mind-reader Fräulein Marlene, who seemed to know all her personal details, was in fact her husband. The 'reveal' was a sensation and there was uproar when Jeremy appeared. It was a brilliant scam immaculately executed. Alan was justifiably proud of himself. *And we of him.*

trained to become a 'performance class' drag act. He was given tuition in the finer points of 'drag artistry' by the professional drag artiste, Terry La Tour. He was also given lessons in movement by a professional choreographer, Nikki Hinkley, and singing lessons by musical director Laurie Holloway, before prerecording a 'backing track' to mime to on the night.

But the drag training was only part of a much more complex operation. Steve needed a dress, tights, shoes, jewellery, a wig, the diadem mask and special contact lenses to disguise his very recognizable pale blue eyes. Steve would eventually have to pluck his eyebrows and shave his legs! But not until the night of the performance – otherwise his wife would almost certainly have suspected something!

THE BIRTH OF A QUICKIE

THE GREAT WORM HUNT

As much thought goes into a 'quickie' as any of the more elaborate set-ups. A good quickie is a very simple practical joke that can be played upon a series of passers-by. A classic was 'Pavement Worms' 'Wouldn't it be funny,' mused Jeremy, 'if we could get people searching for pavement worms?'

Seeing the joke, the programme associate added: 'Because all their tunnelling is causing the paving stones to wobble.'

'That's it,' replied Jeremy.

Added a researcher: 'It really would be a scream if we could get punters listening for the worms with a stethoscope!'

Gleefully, the team developed a seemingly plausible scenario. An actor would pose as a surveyor trying to plot the extent of the tunnelling worms. A Danish heart physician, Doctor Viggurs, fell for

the scam completely and used his professional expertise with a stethoscope to listen for the worms! Could he hear them running along the tunnels? 'Nej!' Could he hear the young ones squeaking? 'Nej!' Could he attract them to the surface by making worm noises? 'Nej!' The good doctor tried very hard, but, unsuspectingly, gave one of the comedy performances of the series.

(Nej is pronounced as 'Nye', by the way. Not a lot of people know that (and even less care)

WORDS NEVER USED IN THE 'BEADLE'S ABOUT' OFFICE

'It was my idea!'

MORE WORDS NEVER USED IN THE *BEADLE'S ABOUT* OFFICE

'VICTIM'

Beadle's About is a comedy show where members of the public unwittingly become comedy actors. We make people STARS!

Rosina Wells
('Personal Parking Barrier')
Series III.

Richard Wharton
('Archaeological Dig')
Series III.

Ron Wood
('Garbage Wall')
Series III.

Maureen Ferguson
('Stuff His Job')
Series III.

and the location of the nearest pub.

GETTING INTO GEAR

The next stage of the operation can now begin: the director will visit the location with the researcher and the AP to figure out exactly where and how the cameras will be hidden. If it is a particularly difficult 'shoot' the director will take the cameraman and sound recordist to discuss any problems. Very, very rarely the whole thing has to be abandoned because of the impossibility of hiding the cameras. When this happens, there is much wailing and gnashing of teeth from the disappointed researcher! The location manager will also go on the recce. He will be thinking about transporting, feeding, watering and 'hiding' all the people who will eventually be involved with the shoot. And all this has got to be done secretly.

IS IT 45 OR 55 ACACIA AVENUE?

I THOUGHT IT WAS AZALEA DRIVE?

I CAN'T SEE A THING AND I'M **SUPPOSED** TO BE THE DIRECTOR!

WHO'S STANDING ON MY SHOULDER?

DON'T 'ALF PONG DOWN HERE!

AT FULL SPEED

Now that the basics have been sorted out it is time to turn a storyline into a carefully crafted piece of comedy. It's time for a 'creative' – a session where an idea is brainstormed. Producer, associate producer, researcher and programme associate sit around and develop an idea. A one-line story – say, repossessing the water in somebody's swimming pool – is turned into a multilayered comedy sketch. *Beadle's About* is a comedy show where members of the public unwittingly become comedy actors. And a lot of thought is given to get the punters 'involved' in what's going on. After the 'creative' the programme associate gets to work on the script. This is the basic working document upon which everything is based. Here's a typical script – 'Political Billboard' – one of the funniest scams of the third series. But remember, all the 'facts' are in fact fiction.

POLITICAL BILLBOARD

Revolutionary leader: Glyn Mills
Second Revolutionary: Susie Fugle
Council Man: Jim McManus
Reporter: Jeremy Beadle

Basic scenario:

Linda Bidgood lives with her husband Michael and three children on an estate in Kettering. Her sister, Margaret Ford, has set her up. The Bidgoods are in the process of buying a piece of land adjacent to their house and this is the basis of the scam. Margaret is a dyed-in-the-wool Tory, thinks Maggie's doing a grand job and all that. She's going to return home and discover that her nightmare of a loony left takeover is coming true.

The land she's buying has been compulsorily purchased by the council and, in the interests of political balance in the borough (they helped a

Meet our revolutionaries

The eyesore itself

right-wing group with it's new headquarters so this evens thing up . . .), the local 'Forward with the Revolution' group has been given permission to erect a huge billboard next to her house. Furthermore, they've strewn leaflets everywhere, stacked banners up against her garage and are planning a series of marches from this site to the town hall.

It's the council's idea!

In fact, could they come to some arrangement with her to rent her garage? It'd make a teriffic central planning office for the Great Struggle to come.

The first march starts this Sunday. They were sure she'd want to help so they've included her phone number on the leaflets in case any-

one want to know the exact location of the starting point. And would she mind making tea for the thirsty marchers? And would she mind selling a few copies of the 'Forward with the Revolution' newspaper? She could take them to the pub where she works and sell them there . . . Here's a steward's armband for Sunday . . . thanks for your help . . .

A man from the council arrives. He's very sympathetic. Doesn't approve of this lot at all . . . but then, he's an SDP man himself. However . . . if you want to live in a democracy, you have to pay the price. This is political balance in action. And the council are perfectly within their rights. If they want a piece of land, for whatever purpose, they can take it. Tough!

Jeremy arrives as a reporter. He's got completely the wrong end of the

And they won't back down!

18

stick and thinks that Linda is Kettering's answer to Rosa Luxembourg. Is it true that she's giving all her worldly goods to the group to help the cause? How long has she been a politicized woman?

Jeremy to camera:

How would you feel if you came home to discover that the land outside your house had been given over to a mass rally to launch the revolution? Especially when you thought you'd bought the plot and now discovered that it has been commandeered as the site for a large political billboard! Well, that's what happened to Linda Bidgood when she returned from shopping with her sister . . .

No matter what I say!

Some lines for our Revolutionary Leader:

Looking good, isn't it! A perfect rallying point for the comrades come next Sunday . . .

Well, it's the revolution, isn't it? It's the beginning of the end for Thatcher's Britain. The struggle has begun! We managed to get this site from those bureaucrats on the local council and the poster went up this morning. We're dead chuffed to get it. It gives you and the other residents a real chance to play your part in the revolution.

Now, this march on Sunday . . . here's a leaflet . . . we put your phone number on it in case people want details on how to get here. We knew you'd be keen to help. Anyway, this march . . . they're coming from all over the country and we're gathering here at 8.30 in the

morning and marching on the town hall. You won't mind making some tea and stuff like that for the marchers, will you? It all helps the cause, doesn't it?

Won't they ever listen?

Some lines for our Second Revolutionary:

Is this a new recruit? Welcome to the movement! We need more sisters involved in the great struggle . . . break the male hegemonist monopoly.

Has Trevor given you a badge? Good . . . I'm Sacha, by the way. I'm in charge of crêche facilities for Sunday. Do you have children? Great! Then you can take charge of the youth. There'll be between fifty and one hundred . . . potential fighters in the revolution to come!

Some lines for our Council Official:

Mrs Bidgood? Ah, I'm glad you're here. You obviously got the letter about the purchase of this land. No . . . I'm sure you did . . .

Yes, well, I'm afraid that the council has placed a compulsory purchase order on this site. It's all in the interests of democracy, you see. I may not share the views of these people but they do have the right to spread their message, don't they? I'm not a political animal myself . . . I voted SDP last time out. David Owen's a good chap, isn't he? . . .

Well, it's political balance. The council did give a grant to 'Freedom from the Taxation Burden' campaign to help them with their new headquarters . . . these people pointed out that we could hardly be seen to be favouring one particular point of view. So, we've donated this site and the cost of erecting the billboard to their organization.

I'm sorry, madam, but I don't like your attitude. I'm afraid that we are the council and we can do what we like. This site has been requisitioned for use by the 'Forward with the Revolution' group and that's that . . .

There's no use complaining . . . there's nothing you or I can do about it. Well, vote them out next time if you don't like it . . .

Some lines for Jeremy as the reporter:

Excuse me . . . I'm from the (*local paper name*) and I wondered if I could have a few words. It's going to make quite a story! Local woman joins revolutionary group!

How long have you been a member of the 'Forward with the Revolution' group? Is it true that you're selling all your belongings and donating the proceeds to the organization.

What made you become a politicized woman? Is this a protest at the forthcoming poll tax? Is it true that you'll be at the head of the march next Sunday?

What does your husband think of all this? Is he a member of the group too?

Thank goodness it's Beadle!

MAKING IT HAPPEN

Getting a funny idea and working it into a funny script is the easy bit. The difficult bit is making it happen. Now it's time to put production flesh on the script bones. And this is how it's done – in discussions with the producer, the associate producer will set the following in train.

CASTING

The actors are cast for the various parts – 'stroppy' council official, peeved Telecom engineer, confused Arab, etc. The contracts are issued by the casting director who is also responsible for supplying 'new faces' for each series. But over the years a 'repertory' group of actors has formed. In one disguise or another they are the series 'regulars'. A script is sent to each actor involved in the scam.

WARDROBE

Costumes for each 'part' are organized via the costume designer. The costume designer will discuss with the producer every aspect of each character's costume. Contrary to popular belief actors very rarely wear their own clothes. In fact, attention to costume detail is absolutely vital. It is simply not on having a policeman wearing hush puppies or brogues – they have to be black Doc Martens. All the information regarding the sizes of the actors involved is passed to the costume designer by the stage manager.

GRAPHICS

The stage manager is also responsible for all the graphics required for each 'scam' – forged documents, etc.

DESIGN

If the story requires large props – say, a 30-foot tree being lowered by crane into a person's front drive – then the designer is consulted. The designer is also responsible for designing and building the various camera 'hides' used during the course of the series. A good 'hide' simply will not be noticed.

PROPS

All 'small props' are organized by the stage manager via the properties' buyer. These can vary from a few potted plants to an elephant.

THE FILMING SCHEDULE

The actual filming of a *Beadle's About* scam is an enormously complex operation and the organizational hub of it all is the location manager. It's the location manager's job to reconcile the fact that the film unit have got to eat with the fact that the 'hit' may have to be done at lunch time.

LAST MINUTE CHANGES

A few days before the shoot the completed script is sent to Jeremy. He will read it and 'phone through any suggestions for strengthening the storyline or 'tweaking' the comedy. This is part of the on-going creative relationship between Jeremy, the producer and the production team. Changes are never a problem because the programme associate writes all the scripts on a word processor.

FINAL PREPARATIONS

Immediately prior to all *Beadle's About* shoots a planning meeting is held. The key people associated with the hit are required to attend this meeting. At the planning meeting, all aspects of the hit are systematically cross-checked, from whether a 'customs officer's' tunic has the correct type of buttons to who is going to 'spot' the punter as he approaches his house – our 'location.' One single mistake could alert the punter to the fact that he or she is on the end of a very elaborate joke. The basic working principle is: if it can possibly go wrong it will – so plan for it!

'TWEAKING THE COMEDY' – AN EVERYDAY STORY OF EVENTS AND FOLK IN THE *BEADLE'S ABOUT* OFFICE

'CASTING' JEREMY

I call it REVENGE!

This is the bit the production team really love – casting Jeremy! Jeremy normally acts (?!?!) as a character in each scam to add another layer of comedy prior to the actual reveal. Here are some of the characters devised by the production team for their star!

Francis Gainsborough: landscape gardener in the swimming pool scam.

Mechanic Beadle: in 'Awful Respray'

Stavros Beadle: the kebab shop owner in 'Crockery Smash'

Uncle Percy: in 'Garden Gnomes'

Wheel's Beadle: the greasy biker in 'Caravan Occupation'

'Rubbish' Beadle: the workman with the rubbish in 'Garbage Wall'

ANOTHER WORD NEVER USED IN THE *BEADLE'S ABOUT* OFFICE

imm

impp

impoo

imposss

impossa

impossn

imposse

imposso

impossii

impossibbb

impossib

impossibll

impossiball?

Nobody knows how to spell it, let alone pronounce it!

JEREMY'S LEAST CONVINCING DISGUISE

?

21

BEADLE'S ABOUT

A NOT VERY CONVINCINGLY COSTUMED CHARACTER FOR A
BEADLE'S ABOUT SCAM

'ELLO 'ELLO! WOT 'AVE WE 'ERE?

SPOT THE TEN ERRORS

1. Hat too small
2. Designer stubble and smoking
3. Floral tie
4. Sergeant's stripes upside down
5. Wrong sort of belt
6. White Lanyard
7. Epaulettes
8. Swagger stick
9. Hush puppies or sneakers
10. Trousers tucked into bright red socks

HELPFUL HINT! If you turn this page over and hold it up to the light you should be able to see the faces!

BEADLE'S ABOUT

THE ACTORS

H ere is a group photo of *all* the actors and actresses ever used in *Beadle's About*. See if you can recognize any of them!

When you have identified all the backs of heads write your answers on a postcard and send them to the *Beadle's About* office. The first correct entry will win an autograph of one of the anonymous actors!

A RARE PHOTO OF BRILLIANTLY DISGUISED CAMERA HIDES

S ee if you can spot the three hidden cameras.

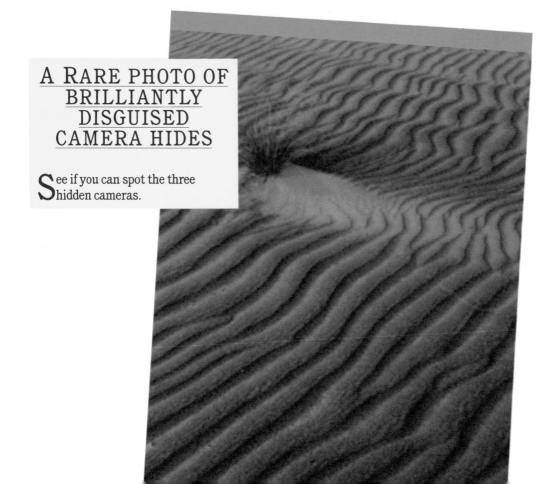

THE DAY OF THE HIT

The plot is thickened

handwritten: After a very late night

handwritten: But for a nominal fee ...

handwritten: and wearing a blindfold —

Cameras, sound and the prop vehicles make their own way to the rendezvous – usually a pub or hotel within a mile or so of the location. Bleary-eyed, the rest of the crew – production team, actors, wardrobe and make-up – arrive from LWT in *very* early morning location transport.

At the rendezvous the final script preparations are made. Jeremy and the producer discuss the storyline with the actors and make suggestions for lines of dialogue, etc. All the actors realize one clear fact: they must not *try* to be funny; they must play it straight and let the comedy come from the punter's *reaction* to the situation.

Concealing the cameras

All the 'entrance' and 'exit' cues are discussed in great detail. The actor playing the part of the 'man from the council' mustn't enter the scene until the 'man from Telecom' has driven off in his van. Or, say, the actor playing the part of a policeman mustn't exit until the 'man from the tax office' arrives. It is vital that each actor knows the storyline backwards – because if it all starts to go wrong they will have to think on their feet! Jeremy and the actors will

rehearse the basic story with the researcher, say, playing the part of the punter. Even the producer is roped in for this! Again, everybody assumes that the punter will not do as expected so they plan accordingly. Acting in *Beadle's About* is like driving a car using only the rear-view mirror!

While the producer and Jeremy are working with the actors the director will be supervising the concealment of the cameras. (And for obvious reasons no photos of this can be included!) The designer will be putting the final touches to, say, the sewage sub-pumping station being placed in somebody's back garden.

Ever seen a back garden sewage station before?

With cameras set to satisfaction the director returns to the 'outside rehearsals'. The story will then be acted through once more for the

benefit of the director. The director will then explain to the actors where the cameras are hidden. It is crucial that the actors keep the punter in an area where he or she can be seen on camera. It sounds obvious, but lots of punters in a state of animation run around like scalded cats making life difficult for the cameramen! An out-of-focus shot of a back of a head is not very much use in telling a story. To their immense professional credit *Beadle's About* directors never miss that all-important close-up.

handwritten: And live to tell the tale

MIKING UP

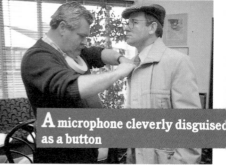

A microphone cleverly disguised as a button

The talking has to stop now. The situation has been discussed in great detail and all possibilities have been planned *and* rehearsed. Now it is time to 'mike up' the actors. Getting clean shots of the punter is one thing, but actually *hearing* what they say is just as important. Each actor is equipped with a minute and very sensitive microphone to pick up what the punter is saying. The sound recordist may have also hidden a number of microphones in various parts of the location – and you would be surprised how microphones can be disguised! It is even possible to secretly mike the inside of a punter's car so that we can actually hear what is said when he or she first sees the, say, pylon in the front garden! But these professional tricks must remain secret. It is to the eternal credit of the sound crew that no picture has ever been lost because there was no sound to go with it.

EXPERTLY CONCEALED HIDES ON A *BEADLE'S ABOUT* SHOOT

MOVING OUT

About half an hour before the time of the hit the entire team moves towards the location. It is the production team's constant nightmare that a punter might arrive early. An enormous amount of organizational effort is put into ensuring that the punter arrives 'on cue'. This may have involved the punter's boss, friends or other members of the family. Today, Bert Hambidge arrives home for lunch to find that his wife, Donna, is having problems with the water board. 'Swimming Pool' is about to be put in the can!

THE HIT

Everybody is hidden in the various camera hides or in nearby houses. Nervous and lonely, the actors posing as 'men from the water board' wait for the punter to arrive. 'Spotters' along the punter's homeward route radio reports to the producer and director. The producer sits with the director and the production assistant in one of the camera hides.

He'll be with you in thirty seconds!

Why ?!?!

Usually acting (?!?!) in the scam, Jeremy is in a 'safe house' with any of the other actors who may be intro- duced as the story develops. The producer, director and Jeremy are in constant radio contact. Tension mounts. A spotter radios that 'the punter is about to turn into the road'.

Sitting in front of the 'video assist' monitors, the director orders the cameras to 'turn over'. The video assist monitors, two small TV sets connected to two cameras, allow the directors to see the overall action.

Dangerous

This is the really dangerous bit. If the punter 'susses the wind-up' then the scam has failed completely and thousands of pounds will have been wasted. Producer and director glance at each other. Crunch time approaches. Will the punter 'buy it'? There is a deathly hush in the camera hides. Only the slight hum of the film cameras can be heard. But seconds before the punter arrives there is a cloudburst. It is so bad that the cameras can barely see anything through the torrential rain. 'Is somebody trying to tell us something?' observes the producer, drily.

This is an unusual example of the producer's WIT!

The punter arrives at his home to find 'men from the water board' removing the water from his swimming pool. This is rather more of a problem than it seems because the outward pressure of the water stops the pool from collapsing inwards! Since the pool cost over £20,000 to build, the punter can foresee a very expensive problem! His first words are: 'what the {bleep} is going on here? Why the {bleep} are you taking the {bleep} water out of my swimming pool?' Suddenly, one of our four men from the water board replies: 'Because we don't want it in there!' This outrages the punter even more: 'for {bleep's} sake!' he explodes.

What the {bleep} is happening here?

In one of the camera hides, the producer and the director exchange smiles – the punter has 'bought it', hook, line and sinker. But there is still a long way to go. It is important to extract every ounce of comedy from the situation. The punter is practically incoherent with rage. First he must stop our two work men from removing the water from his pool. But, in fact, by a very clever design trick the water from the mains is being pumped out and *not* that from the swimming pool! But the punter doesn't know that. He angrily stamps about trying to switch off the pump.

It's time to 'wind-up' the punter a little bit more. Producer and director decide to 'cue-in' a 'senior engineer' from the water board to explain 'the problem' to the enraged owner of the swimming pool. The punter is emphatic that the water board 'has

A VERY RARE PHOTO OF A VERY INCONSPICUOUS SPOTTER AT WORK

THE PUNTER IS ON HIS WAY !

The man from the water board explains

WHAT THE WORD BLEEP! ACTUALLY MEANS
(not to be read by children!)

To find out the exact list of words ever bleeped on *Beadle's About* please turn to page 843.

You are not going to wreck my pool!

no 'bleep' rights to go 'bleep' ruining people's swimming pools'. But the senior engineer enrages the punter even more by insisting that 'the work has got to be done'.

'Idiots'

In the master camera hide, producer, director, production assistant and cameraman can barely hide their mirth as the punter storms around his garden wailing at 'the 'bleep' idiots from the water board'. But things are moving along with an almost mathematical precision. The production assistant keeps an expert eye on exactly how much film is left on each of the three hidden cameras.

Jeremy, the producer and director plan their strategy on a walkie-talkie link. They decide to let the situation 'play' for a while before introducing the next layer of confusion.

Meanwhile, our punter is at total loggerheads with our 'senior engineer'. Our punter simply cannot

understand why water in a swimming pool should affect the mains pressure. And, of course, he is right! But our engineer blandly asserts that the swimming pool owner 'simply doesn't understand the problem'. This is like waving a red flag at a bull.

Please co-operate

Our punter demands to speak to an even more senior man at the water board. This has been anticipated at the planning meeting. Our

engineer produces a mobile phone and proceeds to phone 'head office'. Not fifty yards away another actor answers the 'phone and pretends to be a senior executive from the water board. He asks our punter to 'please co-operate with the men on site'. Our punter can barely believe his ears. The world was a sane place ten minutes ago but now it has gone totally mad!

But there is more madness to come. A decision is made to cue-in the irate 'Telecom engineer' who's

Now Bert is getting the blame for a flooded telecom hole down the road

hole is full of water! Yet another layer of confusion! Our Telecom engineer enters and more or less accuses the punter of being personally responsible for allowing the water to fill his hole. Everybody agrees that it is the punter's fault because, after all, it is his water. The punter no longer knows whether he is coming or going.

But there is yet another complication: one 'Francis Gainsborough'. In this scam Jeremy plays the part of a slightly dotty landscape gardener who has got soaked to the skin from an exploding water mains nearby. Barely able to control their laughter, producer and director cue-in 'Francis'.

Peeling off disguise

Still arguing with the 'senior executive' from the water board our punter simply *doesn't* see through Jeremy's disguise. In fact, he tries to enlist Jeremy's help in stopping

Trying to be reasonable

'the {bleep!} idiots from the water board from {bleep} up my swimming pool!'

Not over yet

Jeremy turns away to peel off his false beard. Still completely bamboozled by it all, our punter still does not recognize 'Francis Gainsborough' for who he really is. It is only when Jeremy waves the mike beneath our punter's nose that he realizes that he has been had. And his reaction? {'BLEEP'}

But things are not finished yet. One of the sound recordists emerges and claps loudly to create sound/vision 'sync' points for each of the cameras used on the shoot. This is vital to edit the film.

The scam now over, the entire production team emerges from their various hidden positions. There is definitely a skittish air about the place, as the hit has been an immense success. And perversely, it has *just* stopped raining!

In all this relaxed chaos, the director has to get essential 'cutaways' – close-up shots of actors, the punter, essential props, etc. It is also time to do Jeremy's 'to camera intro' since it is impossible to do it before the hit or secrecy would be compromised – half the neighbourhood could be hanging out of their windows watching a supposedly secret scam.

and this really, really HURTS!

Thank goodness it's him

CORPSING

It is virtually impossible not to laugh during some of the hits. The actors' professional training steels them against corpsing but Jeremy is notoriously prone to 'go'.

In 'Security Guard Switch' Irene Philipson was looking at a 'wanted' photo of Jeremy. Would she recognize the man showing her the photo? Jeremy almost gave the game away!

THE TEN MOST COMMONLY USED WORDS WHEN JEREMY 'REVEALS'

1. Well I'm . . . bleep!

2. bleep! . . . me

3. Its bleep! Beadle!

4. bleep! you Beadle!

5. bleep! off!

6. I very nearly bleep! you!

7. Whose bleep! idea was this?

8. I knew some bleep! was trying to wind me up

9. I feel a right bleep!

10. You bleep!

AN 'INTRODUCTORY' COCK-UP

'One-take Beadle' prides himself on never having to repeat a 'to camera intro'. But on one occasion he simply couldn't get it right. It was the intro to a scam called 'Mr Maestro Says It's a Fake'. The basic idea was that when a woman came to pick up her Maestro from servicing our 'mechanics' would tell her that it was a fake made in Taiwan. The intro ended with the words, 'Ah so, fiendishry clever oriental plot'. In 'pidgin English' this should have been pronounced, 'Ah so, fiendishry crever oliental prot!' Jeremy simply *couldn't* get it out without corpsing. Gradually, it got to the team. Everytime he ever approached the phrase people would start sniggering. And in turn that sent Jeremy off. Getting a bit exasperated, the

producer tried banning the entire team from the area with the exception of one cameraman. But then the producer started laughing, too. It was never successfully recorded and will, somehow, have to be done as a voice-over!

And I still can't do it!

29

By the way! I never did get it back!

THE QUICKIE

But it is still only lunch time and so it is possible to make yet another film in the afternoon! A 'quickie' has been scheduled in a nearby shopping precinct. The joke is very simple: a pound coin is super-glued to the ground! Unaware that they are being filmed, people go to unbelievable lengths to get the coin!

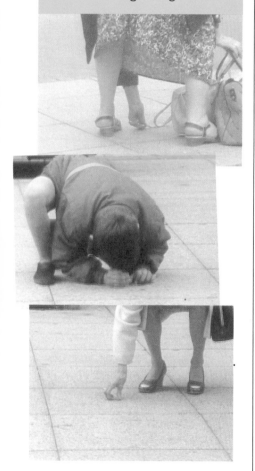

CLASSIC QUICKIES

'THE SUDDENLY MOVING £5 NOTE'

A very fine piece of fishing line was attached to a crispy fiver. As passers-by made to pick up the note it suddenly shot away!

'YOUR FLIES ARE UNDONE!'

As male punters (obviously!) passed our agent provocateur they were told that 'your flies are undone'. The reactions were hysterical.

'THERE'S SOMETHING ON YOUR...'

As passers-by passed our agent provocateur – an actor – he simply said: 'There's something on your backside!'

People then did all manner of contortions trying to locate the 'something'.

'STAVROS'

One of our actors posed as a foreign gentleman having language difficulties with the Passport Office. One passer-by got quite irate trying to explain to the man that he had filled in 'the wrong form'. It was like trying to get blood *into* a stone!

'THE COMMON MARKET CHIP'

Patrons of a Catford chip shop were asked to submit their chips to a range of tests to see whether they would meet the new 'Common Market Requirements'. They were even asked to test the chips' 'bounciness' – no kidding!

'TELEPHONE TESTING'

Our 'engineer' asked passers-by to test a new mobile 'phone for 'reception'.

SIMPLE PRACTICAL JOKES

Sometimes the simplest practical jokes make the funniest scams. Here's a photo selection of the very best practical jokes from *Beadle's About*.

Mobile Wig – simply a moving wig to embarrass people at an inter view.

Exploding Golf Balls – self-explanatory.

Antique Disasters – furniture in an antique shop was rigged to fall apart if you so much as looked at it.

Al Goshman's Balls – a trick case that falls open.

PERMISSIONS

Nowadays in hidden camera comedy any person who has appeared must first have given their permission. This means that on a 'quickie' shoot the researchers may have to sprint all over the place to catch people before they disappear into shops or buses, into stations, etc. Very, very few people refuse permission to show film shot by the *Beadle's About* team. But the *Beadle's About* team do not believe in blackmail.

LOOKS OF HORROR

When punters blunder into a *Beadle's About* scam you can expect to see all sorts of expressions cross their faces. Here is a gallery of now famous faces.

'Boxing Match'

'Personal Parking'

'Yellow Lines'

'Austin 7 Removal'

'Dog Loo'

'Flood'

'Stuff His Job'

'Spare Parts Club'

'Collapsing Bed II'

'Political Billboard'

'Car Valet'

'French Parking'

The main reason why people refuse to give permission is that they are with somebody they shouldn't be with.

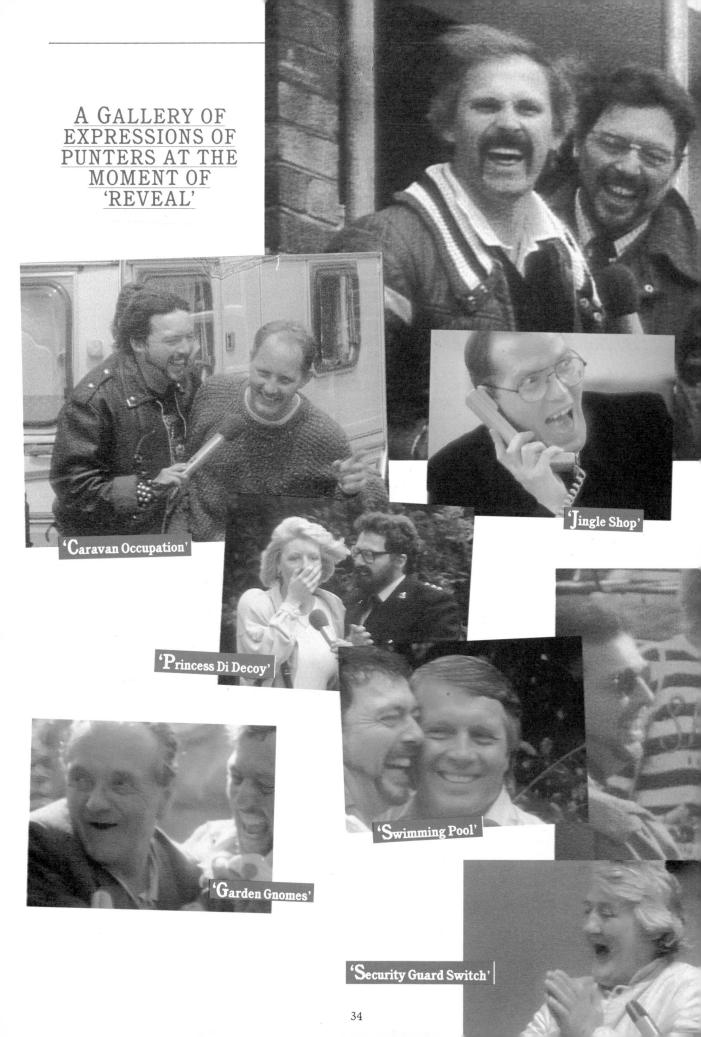

A GALLERY OF
EXPRESSIONS OF
PUNTERS AT THE
MOMENT OF
'REVEAL'

'Caravan Occupation'

'Jingle Shop'

'Princess Di Decoy'

'Swimming Pool'

'Garden Gnomes'

'Security Guard Switch'

BEADLE'S ABOUT

'Bricked-up Balcony'

'Crockery Smash'

'Political Billboard'

'Frascati Fiddle'

'Metal Detector'

'Monster Smash'

'Collapsing Bed'

'Hurricane Tree Replacement'

DIFFERENT REACTIONS TO DISASTER

FLYING SAUCERS!

With certain types of scam it is possible to play them on a number of punters. The 'Great Crockery Smash' was such a wind-up.

The set-up was very simple. An in-on-the-joke husband would return from a 'surprise' lunch with his wife to find that his car had been boxed in by a van. Conveniently, the keys would be left in the van's ignition. With the help of his wife he would back-up the van to create space to move their car. But backing-up the van would trigger a disaster – thousands of pieces of crockery would be propelled into the middle of the road! The wife would then get the blame for encouraging her husband into the ill-advised initiative. The joke was played upon Lee Mirams and Jacqueline Urden. Both became stars of two very funny stories. But their very first reactions to the moment of disaster were completely different!

TELLING FIBS

Sometimes, punters are lured into the most extreme situations – and they can only get themselves out of trouble by taking the most extreme actions. Take Helen Brugger. She was sent along to 'temp' in what seemed to be a perfectly straightforward office. But things are never what they seem to be when Beadle's at the bottom of things! Let the story unfold.

On arriving the boss told Helen that he was taking a long weekend to Paris. Before going to collect some travellers' cheques he asked Helen to confirm the flight bookings and wrap a very expensive-looking fur coat. Soon after the boss had disappeared to the bank a young lady entered the office – evidently the boss's romantic connection! She was delighted to be going to Paris and, yes, the fur coat was *supposed* to be a surprise!

Woman in cupboard

A 'phone call interrupted the girls' chat – it was the boss saying that he had to return to pick up his chequebook. The girlfriend would hide in a cupboard and spring a little surprise of her own! No sooner had she hid in a cupboard than another woman arrived. She wished to see her husband – our boss. And she wished to know all about the air tickets *and* the fur coat. Helen played dumb, stonewalling everything with a bland, 'er . . . I don't know'.

Eventually the boss arrived to pick up his chequebook. And Helen had to explain that not only had the wife turned up unexpectedly but that there was another woman in the cupboard! Things rapidly came to a head when the wife went to the cupboard to hang up her overcoat! Helen moved swiftly to avoid disaster. She took the wife's coat to hang in the cupboard. But imagine her surprise when she discovered not the girlfriend but Jeremy Beadle!

'THE MISTRESS' – EDITED HIGHLIGHTS

Our boss explains that he is off to Paris for the weekend.

Helen is left to check the flights and wrap the fur coat.

Enter the girlfriend!

The boss rings. He is about to return.

Helen and the girlfriend soon make friends. Isn't the fur coat lovely?

The girlfriend decides to spring a surprise. She hides in a wardrobe.

Who's this?

The boss's wife!

The boss returns. How is he going to get out of this appalling mess?

The wife goes to the cupboard.

Helen can see disaster looming.

The reveal.

Sean Connery gets Japan. Roger Moore gets India. I get the inside of a dusty cupboard in Waterloo.

VERY NEARLY A WASHOUT

People often ask: Do any of the stories fail? The answers are: Yes. Nearly. Once!

For a long time an American-inspired idea had been discussed in the office. The idea was this: we would put a yellow line where one had not previously existed – and *over* somebody's car, to boot. The problem had always been finding a location *and* the punter to go with it. The problem had defeated a number of researchers. Alan Hopkins suddenly produced a solution to the problem. In his New Malden Road a 'situation' was in the making. The local council had put a double yellow line down *one* side of the road and the residents were most concerned about the lines being put on *both* sides – i.e., outside their houses. One punter in particular was very angry at the very thought of this: Jan White. By bringing other members of her family in on the conspiracy the following 'plot' was agreed: Jan would arrive home

from shopping to find a double yellow line outside her house and *right* over the *top* of her son's new black Volkswagen Passat. It was confidently predicted that Jan would 'blow'.

There was one obvious problem with the story: we would have to use paint that could be washed off with water. But what would happen if it started to rain *just* before the scam started. The 'joke' would literally go down the drain. But a decision was made to go ahead with the idea and hope that it wouldn't rain on the day. You've got to be optimistic to do this show.

The organizational run-up to the day went very smoothly: arrangements were made to get Jan out of her house while preparations were made. It had been organized for Jan to be out at 9.00 am and to return at 1.00 pm.

The day before the hit, thick dark clouds started scudding in from the south-west. Ominous. And on the morning of the hit it poured down! There was no way yellow lines could be put on the road or across the top of her son's car. Eventually the black Passat was taken to a nearby multi-story car park to have the yellow lines painted on. It was then driven back to the location wrapped in clear plastic sheeting. At noon it was still pouring down. By extremely deft

footwork, arrangements were made to keep Jan away until 2.00 – that gave another two hours for the rain to ease off. At 1.30 it stopped raining. But the road was still wet.

No Jan

The road was covered with dust sheets and paper to absorb the wetness. At 1.45 a strip of road was dry enough to 'paint' with the yellow lines. At 1.56 the lines either side of the car were completed. The plastic sheeting was whipped off the car. At 1.57 everything was ready. And the rain was holding off.

But at 2.00 Jan did not appear! She had missed a bus. By more extremely deft footwork it was established that Jan would arrive at 2.20 exactly. All concerned anxiously watched the now darkening sky. But still the rain held off. These were particularly tense moments for Alan Hopkins – then the stage manager on *Beadle's About* – because he had researched and set up the story in the hope of succeeding to a forthcoming research job. At 2.17 a spotter reported that Jan had got off the bus and was heading for her road. And precisely at that moment the heavens opened! Within seconds the carefully painted yellow lines were being sluiced down the drains! Alan looked desolate – he could see his career prospects going the same way. The producer mumbled: 'I really am very sorry that it's turned out this way, Alan.'

The producer then wandered off confident in the knowledge that the whole enterprise was a complete washout in every sense of the word. He passed the black Passat – the painted cardboard line stuck on the car was *just* about holding up. Within seconds Jan had hurried to the scene. 'What the bleep hell have you done to my son's car'! she yelled. Against all the odds it was going to work. And two days later, Alan successfully applied for the research job.

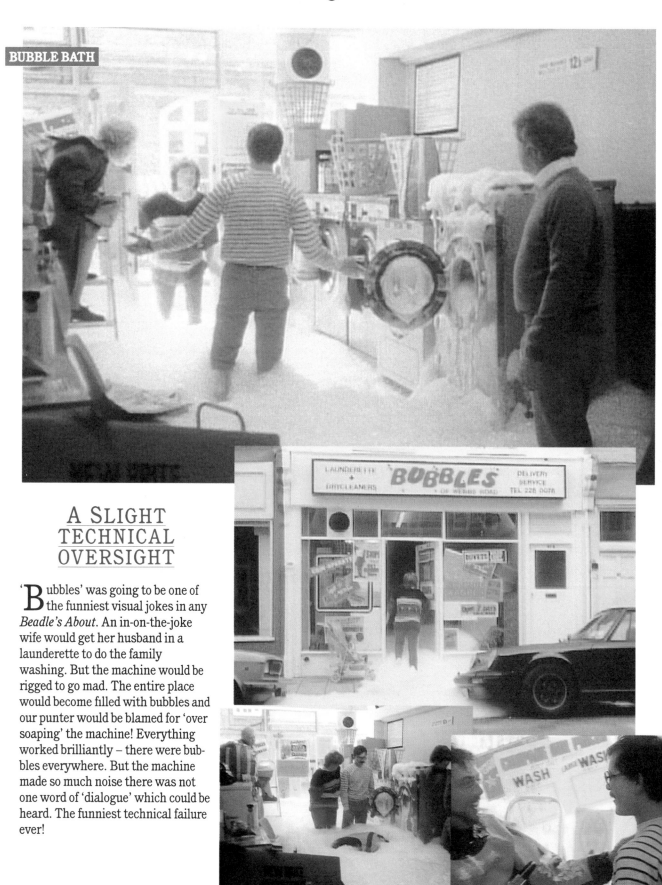

BUBBLE BATH

A SLIGHT TECHNICAL OVERSIGHT

'Bubbles' was going to be one of the funniest visual jokes in any *Beadle's About*. An in-on-the-joke wife would get her husband in a launderette to do the family washing. But the machine would be rigged to go mad. The entire place would become filled with bubbles and our punter would be blamed for 'over soaping' the machine! Everything worked brilliantly – there were bubbles everywhere. But the machine made so much noise there was not one word of 'dialogue' which could be heard. The funniest technical failure ever!

NEARLY ANOTHER DISASTER!

The very last shoot of the very first series of *Beadle's About* was very nearly a total disaster.

The team had received a letter from Terri Hayes who wanted to set up her brother-in-law Derek. Derek lived near to a water works and an underground reservoir in Frinton-on-Sea. The plot was simplicity itself: the local 'water board' would excavate beneath the floor of Derek's lounge in order to locate an original 'junction point'. Once located, the piping would be extended from beneath Derek's house to the site of a proposed trout farm. This would mean digging up Derek's front garden, too. But worse was to come. For the duration of the work Derek and his family would have to move into temporary accommodation. And all this the day before the family were due to fly off for a Mediterranean holiday!

Catastrophic results

The organization would be relatively straightforward because Derek would be out of the house by 9 am on the dot. And there would be no danger of him arriving home from work early. On Fridays, traffic warden Derek would *always* spend the morning in nearby Walton-on-the-Naze before returning home for lunch at 1 pm prompt. But on this Friday Derek decided to do his duties as a traffic warden in Frinton-on-Sea – with nearly catastrophic results. Because he decided to patrol the area not a stone's throw away from his house!

The team first knew of this change of plan when they saw Derek arrive outside their café rendezvous and book the PA's car for being illegally parked! The rest of the morning was a nail-biting affair. But, fortunately, Derek didn't patrol his own road and disaster was averted. And, on cue at 1 pm, he became ensnared in one of the best scams ever.

This wasn't here when I left for work!

Look what's going on here!

Who are you?

An Englishman's home is his castle

The P.A. thought it was another of my 'little jokes'.

without using mirrors....

THE GREATEST EVER FAILURE

The most heroic failure ever was 'Forty Ford Fiestas'. Set up by her brother, Christine Stamford left her new red Ford Fiesta in what seemed to be an ordinary car park. When she returned the car park was choc-a-bloc with spanking new, red Ford Fiestas! She had found herself in the middle of a Ford Fiesta sale. But how would Christine locate her car? The problem was complicated by the fact that the Beadle team had taken her registration plates and affixed them to another car. They had taken all her knick knacks and put them in another car! Christine would *never* be able to locate her pride and joy! What a wheeze!

Setting up the scam was a logistical nightmare. How do you hide thirty-nine bright red cars? The problem was solved by hiding them in a field behind a very large nearby building. Christine duly parked her car. As soon as she had disappeared the other cars were removed and the thirty-nine Ford Fiestas were wheeled in. Then came the dressing – the bunting, the sales banners, etc. By the time Christine returned to the car park the scene was convincingly set.

And what were Christine's first words?

WHERE'S JEREMY BEADLE, THEN ?

THE SCAM HAD FAILED!
It was one of the most spectacular failures ever shot on hidden cameras.

BUT EVERY CLOUD HAS A SILVER LINING

How Philip Wiltshire's car got a complete respray:

Gail and Roy Wiltshire wrote to the *Beadle's About* team about their son Philip who was obsessively attached to his car – a slightly ageing Vauxhall Cavalier. Could they think of a trick to play on Philip? It wasn't long before a scam emerged: unbeknown to Philip the car would be taken to a local garage to be resprayed as a birthday present from his parents. But the respray would go hideously wrong and the car would end up as a blotched mess. And it would be Philip's fault for using the wrong kind of 'polyacetate polish' prior to the respray! The reveal would come when Jeremy, disguised as a mechanic, would wash off the blotched paint to reveal the original, even colour.

Botched job

Technically, it was quite simple to do a 'botched' job on Philip's car. The car would be painted and 'blotched' with water colour. Then a layer of water soluble lacquer would be applied to make it look as if the car had been resprayed with real, oil-based paint. Conveniently, the whole thing would wash off with hot water.

The scam was played with enormous success. Philip got very angry about his badly blotched pride and joy. And the reveal worked perfectly.

There was only one problem. As a result of some totally unforseen chemical reaction between the hot cleansing water, the lacquer, the water colour paint *and* the original colour, *real* blotches formed! The end result was that the car had to be stripped back to the metal before being completely resprayed – this time for real!

And guesswho got the blame for THIS!

RESPRAY BLUES

What blotch?

That blotch!

What blotch?

That blotch!

AN ORGANIZATIONAL NIGHTMARE

Here comes our first couple, Jay and Ricky Dance – on time to the minute!

Our policeman explains the basic problem to the couple. Will the lady help 'Princess Diana'. The husband is all for helping out.

The actors are in position. Our Princess Di is some way from where the couple will be waved down, thus decreasing the chance that our punter will 'see through the disguise'.

The lady-in-waiting explains the sub-plot: driving the XJS around the nearby lanes.

And an all-time classic! The 'Princess Di Decoy' scam. The idea – developed by comedy director Terry Kinane – was very simple: in essence, female motorists would be asked to stand-in for Princess Di who would be trying to avoid the unwelcome attentions of a French photographer. From this very simple acorn a monumentally complex oak tree grew.

The story developed along the following lines. A couple would be flagged down by a policeman. The policeman would explain that Princess Diana – standing near an XJS Jaguar – was being followed to a 'private engagement' by a particularly bothersome French photographer. Would the lady help out by pretending to be Princess Diana? In on the joke, the husband would encourage his wife to help out. All that our Princess Di stand-in had to do was to drive the Princess's car around some lanes to decoy the French photographer while the real

Princess Di made her escape in the couple's car! The decoy couple would then return the XJS to the start point to wait for the delivery of their car. What could be simpler? But then the whole thing would turn to disaster: another policeman would appear to arrest our helpful lady for 'impersonating Royalty'.

The story-line was ingenious but essentially simple. But actually making it happen was an organizational nightmare! The easy bit was finding an actress to play the part of

Princess Diana – Julie Wooldridge was the most look-alike 'look-alike' for Princess Diana.

Then it was a case of finding a suitable location. It would not be possible to mount a scam of this complexity in Greater London because crowds would automatically gather at the first sighting of somebody who seemed to be Princess Diana. It had to be a deserted country lane where

wanna bet!

TECHNIQUES FOR HIDING PEOPLE ON THE 'PRINCESS DI DECOY' SCAM

A very heavily disguised cameraman.

A very heavily disguised film unit.

At that moment the French photographer arrives to start taking pictures of what he imagines is Princess Di.

The lady goes along with the idea. She gets into Princess Diana's XJS Jaguar.

Decoy Diana drives off with her husband.

A country policeman now appears and wants to know who has illegally parked this car.

The French photographer in hot pursuit.

The Decoy Diana tries to explain what happened – helping Princess Di to escape from a French photographer, etc.

Decoy Diana becomes very angry with these unwelcome attentions.

Apart from miking the car to hear what is being said, the *whole* decoy run was being filmed.

The 'real' Princess Diana, the lady-in-waiting and the policeman drive off in the couple's car.

The country cop simply doesn't believe a word of it. Would you?

The car is then returned to the clearing – and a 'no parking' sign is added to the scene. All this happens seconds before . . . .

The Decoy Diana returns to pick up her own car – now illegally parked.

members of the public could not accidentally become involved in the deception. And, of course, it would be necessary for our decoy couple to be able to drive around in a circle in order to leave the XJS at the start point *and* retrieve their own car.

Private lunch engagement

But where to look for this stretch of deserted road with obliging turn-off points? There would need to be a reason for Princess Diana being in any part of Essex, Kent or Surrey. She would not simply be 'out for a drive'. Eventually, it was agreed that the Princess would be going to one of the Kent castles (Hever, Leeds, Scotney or Penshurst Place) for a 'private lunch engagement'. This enabled the researcher to narrow down the search for the system of roads required. This was done using an ordnance survey map of the area. A number of locations were visited and one finalized.

Finding a husband

At this point the scam had been written, cast and the location had been found. Working out hides for the cameras and hiding all members of our cast were mere formalities. The real problem remained: finding a husband who would guarantee to drive along the selected stretch of road with his wife at a specific time on the decreed day of filming – for reasons of economy always a week-day. This meant that the husband and his wife would need to take time off work. And if they, say, lived in Essex why would they just happen to be motoring through the Kent countryside? Lots of fibs would have to be told by the in-on-the-joke husband! But with a scam of this complexity and, frankly, riskiness, it would be necessary to do it on three separate couples to absolutely *guarantee* a successful result. Even if all three were only patchily funny it would be possible to edit together the 'best bits' to make an item that would repay the enormous costs involved. So the researcher had to find three such couples for the same filming day! Their 'arrivals', then, would have to be staggered. But this would lead to all sorts of problems in re-setting the scene. Accurate arrival times would be vital to the success of the operation – yet another complication for the researcher.

But first the problem of actually finding the punters had to be solved. And this is where the 'readers' letters files came in. Practically every single man who had ever written to *Beadle's About* wanting to play a joke on girlfriend, fianceé or wife

While all this is happening our country cop has called his inspector for 'assistance'.

Jeremy arrives as a police inspector and listens to Decoy Diana's story.

The police inspector, too, doesn't believe a word of it. He warns her that 'impersonating Royalty' is a very serious offence.

Our Decoy Diana is now beginning to get a bit worried.

But finally all is revealed.

was secretly contacted. Many, many calls were made before three couples were found. Then an elaborate 'fib' was prepared for each husband plausibly to explain why they should just happen to be driving through Kent on a Thursday. The husbands were secretly taken to the location, told where to drive in a circle and, of course, given their 'arrival' times.

Decoy Dianas

But the director had his problems, too. Not just hiding an entire film unit in the middle of a deserted country road, but also filming the 'decoy Dianas' as they drove the 'real' Princess's XJS! The XJS would have to be miked up, too, to pick up anything the decoy Dianas would say. Thee was also the problem of 'cueing' the French photographer and his vehicle from another hiding

place. Spotters would also be required to warn of impending arrivals. The whole operation required a 100 per cent reliable communications system – in itself a miracle of ingenuity.

By 11.30 on the day of filming the entire unit was ready in hiding.

'Princess Diana', her 'lady-in-waiting' and an accompanying 'policeman' nervously awaited the arrival of our first decoy Diana. The scene was set for one of the most complex pieces of storytelling ever attempted in the thirty-year history of hidden camera filming. And 9 still don't know how it worked.

46

LOOKING LIKE ROYALTY

PROFFERING THE ROYAL JAFFA

The 'Princess Di Decoy' scam was one of the most complicated pieces of hidden camera filming ever. But 'Royalty' isn't new to the Beadle team. In fact, two scams in the 1987 series featured 'The Queen' and 'Fergie and Andrew' respectively. First, 'The Queen':

The joke was played upon Jean Strachan who worked part-time in a greengrocers'. She was set up by the owner of the shop. Soon after Jean arrived for work a very large limousine with smoked glass windows drew up outside the shop. An immaculately liveried footman emerged from the car leading a number of corgis on leads. It had to be the Queen in the car, had it not? The 'footman' was suitably discreet.

'Could we possibly have a selection of fruit?' he asked. After curtseying to the car Jean offered 'Her Majesty' the selection. A gloved hand emerged from the darkened rear window. But 'Her Majesty' was not at all impressed with the selection and 'she' started throwing apples and oranges in all directions! Jean was rather perplexed by this display of Royal displeasure until the real owner of the gloved hand was revealed. It was Jeremy!

BUMP-STARTING A HELICOPTER!

Heartened by the success of 'The Queen and the Cox's Orange Pippins' the team developed another idea: the 'Royal Helicopter' scam. The basic idea was very simple. Set-up mechanics would be called to the grounds of a hotel to do a 'special emergency job'. They would arrive to find a characteristic *red* Wessex of the Queen's flight. And who would they see on the flight deck? Prince Andrew piloting Fergie to a little birthday bash at Highgrove – home of the Prince and Princess of Wales.

The scam posed two difficulties: finding exact 'look-alikes' for Andrew and Fergie and getting hold of a red Wessex helicopter. A 'look-alike' agency found the 'Royalty' and the Royal Naval Air Service kindly helped out with the Wessex. The scene was set for one of the funniest ever scenes on *Beadle's About* – Frank Clark trying to 'bump start' a helicopter!

CAR JOKES

After your house, your car is probably your most prized possession. Little wonder then that the *Beadle's About* team religiously wrecks a car each series. Here's a selection of car smash stories.

WINGED!

'COURTESY CAR PARKING'

Sue Schlesinger went to have a Chinese meal with her husband, Roger. The restaurant offered a unique 'courtesy car parking service'. While Sue sat down to order, the chauffeur parked her car. But it wasn't 'courtesy' parked at all. It was swapped for another, obviously smashed model. Imagine what Sue said when *this* car was returned to her after the meal!

Sue was mightily relieved to find that her car had been switched!

'TANK CRUSH'

A husband and wife return from looking around a military museum to find they have been blocked in by a Chieftain tank. In on the joke, the husband decided to try to move the tank – with catastrophic consequences.

Joan and husband arrive to find the car has become part of a 'publicity' shoot.

The 'shoot' commences.

'Sky-High' crashes forward and over the first cars.

Joan sees the danger.

Joan fights to save her car!

Joan cannot believe she has witnessed what she has seen or heard what has just been said.

And from Series III:
'MONSTER SMASH'

'Monster Smash' was probably the most spectacular smash-up ever organized by the *Beadle's About* team. The giant 'sky-high' wagon would flatten a punter's car after flattening five others. The first problem was to make an exact duplicate of Joan Bone's car. Then, while she was enjoying the 'World of Adventures' at Chessington with her husband, Dave, a 'photographic publicity shoot' was organized around her car. Joan arrived back on the scene just in time to see 'Sky High' crashing across the tops of cars moving ever nearer to her prized red Escort XR3I Special! Joan practically went mad.

Here are the highlights:

Joan, Just didnt go bananas! She practically went FRUIT SALAD !!

FUNNY PICTURES

Here's a selection of the film editors' favourite 'funny pictures'.

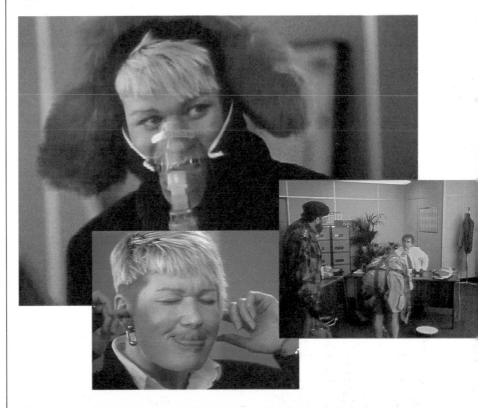

Yet, it can't be true! Jeremy reveals.

A VERY FUNNY PICTURE

Probably the funniest ever sequence of 'funny pictures' to be seen on *Beadle's About*.

EDITING THE FILM

O nce all the film and sound have been put into sync the actual process of editing can begin. This is an awesome task. Since there are usually three but sometimes four cameras running, the editor can be faced with an awful lot of film to be boiled down to a ten-to-twelve minute version. The editor will work from script with the director to make the first 'rough cut'. The unspoken rules on this point are: keep the story logic, but don't lose any laughs *and* keep the funny pictures. Once a satisfactory rough cut has been achieved, another three or four minutes is shaved off to give an eight- or nine-minute 'fine' cut. This version is viewed by the producer who may suggest changes. There is another basic rule of thumb here: if everybody is falling about laughing there can't be that much wrong with the film. Usually, any changes made at this point are 'tweaks' rather than re-cuts. End-of-show or 'finale' items normally leave the cutting rooms at seven to eight minutes' duration.

I certainly wouldn't wish anybody to do something I wouldn't do myself. Mind you, I'd get them to do it first.

THE SCAM

T hree people were invited to a garage to 'test drive' a Montego. Little did they know that the 'spin' in the car would be more than they bargained for! They would be driven by 'Montego' stunt driver, Russ Swift.

THE PUNTERS

Sally-Ann Clingain

Geoff Kilsby

Chris Morgan

BUT WHAT DO THE PUNTERS SAY?

A selection of photos of various punters and what they actually say about being 'Beadled'.

Sally-Ann Clingain ('Wheelies') I'd do it again tomorrow. I really enjoyed it.

Linda Bidgood ('Political Billboard') I wish I'd had one more gin!

Bert Hambidge ('Swimming Pool') While it was happening I believed it was all for real – and my wife had been acting suspiciously. What a relief to know that it was all innocent.

Les Etherton ('Caravan Occupation') I was flabbergasted! It was well done! What a shock when I found out it was Jeremy.

Tony Moroncini ('Frascati Fiddle') Initially, everyone else enjoyed it more than I did but when I realized you weren't really going to confiscate my wine I found it a really good laugh!

Jay Dance ('Princess Di Decoy') I was horrified while it happened! But what a great experience and I enjoyed every moment afterwards.

Owen Andrews ('Garden Gnomes') A lot of people think they wouldn't be caught out but the set up was so clever I fell for it hook, line and sinker!

PUTTING A SHOW TOGETHER

This long and complicated process is required for each of the fifty or so film shots for a series of *Beadle's About*. Now the process of putting the shows together for 'the studio' can begin.

On one wall in the production office all the successful films are represented by cards stuck on a huge board. The producer spends hours staring at this board.

Basically, the contents of each edition of *Beadle's About* are decided by Jeremy, the producer, the AP and the programme associate – the programme associate has, by now, an encyclopaedic knowledge of each film, its duration and, crucially, where the laughs are. On *Beadle's About* the laughs are referred to as 'woofers', 'belters' or 'screamers'. (See Glossary, page 5.) The trick is to pack as many screamers as possible into each show. An unwritten rule is that there should be a *minimum* of four loud laughs per minute of programme. *SCREAMERS, preferable*

VERY RARE SOUND RECORDING TAKEN WHEN PROGRAMME RUNNING ORDERS ARE BEING DISCUSSED

The 'blend' of each show is carefully decided. Strangely, it's usually done backwards! First the 'finale' is decided. Then the 'end of part' – the item that comes before the commercial break. Then the 'opener' is decided. Other items are fitted around these three basic items. During this process lots of the film cards are continually being shuffled around the production board. Since filming continues throughout the period when the shows are recorded – August, September and October – only those films shot in early or mid-summer can be included in the August recordings. But this has never caused any problems and there is an abundance of material to choose from. Once the running orders for the first four shows have been decided the programme associate begins to write the studio 'links'. The links compromise the introduction to the show in the form of the 'video menu', the introduction to each item (the 'intros'), the chat after each item (the 'outros'), the link into the next item and the 'goodnights'.

The films selected for each programme are than transferred to video tape in show order – this way it is possible to get an accurate idea of how long each show will run. At this stage the running length for all the items in the show plus the links should be about twenty-three minutes for a show that will transmit at twenty-four minutes and thirty seconds. The extra one minute and thirty seconds will come from applause and what is mysteriously called 'spread' or 'stretch'. And it is at this point that the now famous 'bleep bubble' is added.

HOW THE BLEEP BUBBLE IS PUT ON THE FILM

The 'bleep' bubble is put over punters' mouths for obvious reasons! But exactly how is it done?

First, a 'graphic' is prepared by the graphics department. This is a straightforward piece of artwork on white cardboard. A photograph is then taken of the artwork and a 35 mm slide is produced. The slide is put into a machine which converts the photographic picture into an electronic picture. Conveniently, this electronic picture can be moved around the picture to be bleeped and its size can be varied.

Here are a selection of pictures bleeped. See if you can guess what was said!

Now guess the word used in each of the pictures and forward your guesses to the *Beadle's About* office. The first correct application received will win a blow bubble set.

BEADLE'S ABOUT

SOME JOLLY GOOD OPENERS OR HOLIDAY COMPLICATIONS

Sometimes the *Beadle's About* team play jokes upon people who are just about to go on holiday. Here's a photo selection of your favourites:

'CLUB 75–90'

Nick Ingleman was asked to take a little old lady on holiday with his girlfriend.

'FATAL ATTRACTION'

Valerie Marsh and Sharon Cromie thought that some blonde from their husband's office had invited herself on their holidays.

'ROWDY MATES'

And Angela May and Jean Barnett were not too pleased when they thought that some long-lost rowdy friends of their husbands would be accompanying them on holiday.

And Janice got really annoyed when she was told that she could not have guacamole more than once a week.

'TUNISIAN MARRIAGES'

Martin Lloyd looked forward to going on holiday with his girlfriend – but not to be forced to get married at Luton Airport to satisfy the strict fundamentalist law of another country.

'THE NEVER-ENDING MENU'

Janice Holloway was looking forward to going on a two-week Mediterranean holiday – but she did not expect to have to specify exactly what she would want to eat on every meal for the entire two weeks.

WHAT ABOUT A SMASH TO END THE PART?

In every series of *Beadle's About* something gets smashed. Here is one of the very best smashes from the three series of *Beadle's About*. From Series I:

'PORTACABIN'

Geoff Hayes, a dealer in second-hand portacabins, was lured to our location to buy one. But something went wrong, and the portacabin 'accidentally' got dropped on a selection of garden gnomes! Guess who everybody tried to blame?

GOLD DIGGERS – A TYPICAL FINALE

O ne of the high points of the '88 series of *Beadle's About* was the 'Metal Detector' scam. Dave Stuckey was set up by his friend Terry Carter to 'discover' some very rare gold coins that had been planted by the *Beadle* team. Dave would then be accused of recovering the hidden loot from the premises of a nearby coin shop.

The stage manager, Stephen Joel, hid eight gold coins (worth about £4,000), in an area of approximately 15 square feet at a depth of about 3 inches. The coins wouldn't be that difficult to find, would they? Terry led his pal to the area where he had previously found a coin – planted by the team, in fact! Both started hunting for gold with their detectors. Inexplicably, they were very difficult to detect and it seemed ages before anybody found anything. But once one coin had been found it wouldn't be too difficult to find the others, would it? But it was. In fact, the director had to stop filming to conserve film stock! Eventually, Dave found some coins and it became possible to complicate matters with the charge of theft. And was Dave relieved when the truth was revealed!

The scam was a great success but another problem arose. Three gold coins worth some £2,000 had to be recovered! It wouldn't be difficult would it? But a very anxious stage manager needed all the help he could get to find those coins!

THERE'S GOLD IN THEM THAR HILLS

ANOTHER FINALE AND AN AMAZING DISPLAY OF ACTING

Sometimes in a *Beadle* set-up the person actually doing the set-up is required to act. Probably the most convincing piece of acting ever seen on *Beadle's About* came from Yvonne Forrest who wanted to set up her son Steven, a Royal Navy sailor and keen boxer. But Yvonne hated the thought of her son acquiring cauliflower ears from boxing so she had the idea of

GOBSMACKED!

Look closely and you'll be able to see Steven's gum shield fall out in amazement.

unexpectedly turning up at one of her son's bouts. The Royal Navy kindly arranged an entire ship vs ship tournament.

Steven had the surprise of his life when his mother turned up and tried to stop the bout. It was a brilliant piece of acting and Steven's look of surprise is probably one of the funniest shots ever seen on *Beadle's About*.

PREPARING FOR THE STUDIO

Once Jeremy has tweaked the links to his satisfaction the production assistant can go ahead with the preparation of the studio script. The studio script is a vitally important document. The studio script will include a complete schedule for the day for all involved; a precise breakdown of all technical requirements and the director's 'camera script' – a complete breakdown of *exactly* what each of the five studio cameras will be looking at at any moment in time.

Each researcher will now start to contact each punter who is to appear on the show – usually family and friends are invited, too. The punter and whoever set them up are asked to wear 'their party best' and to avoid stripes, checks and dots. Stripes, checks and spots 'strobe' – that is, cause an irritating electronic effect on the viewers' television set.

THE STUDIO DAY

While the set is being constructed and the lighting organized, work continues on the script. Jeremy, the producer and the programme associate 'tweak' the links to perfection. The final version is given to the autocue girl. Apart from being a visual aid the autocue enables Jeremy to time the links to the split second.

REHEARSALS

Camera rehearsals begin at 14.30 prompt. Every single shot in the show is rehearsed from the initial 'walkdown' to the final 'goodnights'. Even at this late stage the links are pruned down to the bare bones. As two editions of *Beadle's About* are recorded on each studio day, so two shows are rehearsed for lighting, cameras, sound and stage management. At this point it is possible to time the programmes to the nearest half-second.

OUR STARS ARRIVE

Towards the end of the afternoon rehearsals our stars begin to arrive. They are welcomed and reassured by Jeremy on the set. They are briefly rehearsed as to what's going to happen before being whisked away to relax in 'hospitality'.

THE SHOW IS PUT IN THE CAN

After hospitality the stars are taken to make-up to dab over any shiny noses or perspiring brows. Jeremy has the full slap that will enable him to spend two hours beneath studio lights, without breaking into an obvious sweat.

The studio audience has arrived and are being entertained by the

THE WARM-UP

warm-up man, Bill Martin. A legend in the business, Bill can take an ice-cold audience and work them into a cheerful frame of mind. The producer, who claims to have a 'nose'

for a good audience, prowls around. He reports to Jeremy that it's a 'good crowd and they should "go"' – that is, split their sides laughing at what all believe to be two very funny programmes. Jeremy makes his entrance to tumultuous applause, stamping and whistling. While he jokes with the audience final technical checks are being make. At 7.29 precisely everything is 'ready to roll'. The floor manager conveys the message to Jeremy. He moves to the rear of the set ready to make his 'show' entrance when the titles have been rolled.

Good luck

In the gallery, the studio director routinely wishes everybody good luck. The producer ritually mumbles 'break a leg and don't mention the Scottish play'. 'Roll vt,' the director orders. The show is on the road.

The titles flash up on the gallery monitors, the audience is cued to applaud. The titles end, the director orders a lighting change and Jeremy appears to more thunderous applause. Usually, the studio recording is so well organized and rehearsed it passes in under an hour. This particular recording has been a great success. The studio audience loved every minute of it and the show is choc-a-bloc with an assortment of woofers, belters and screamers. Jeremy is exultant. There are broad grins everywhere. But there is still a long way to go. The second show has still to be recorded.

Between shows Bill Martin entertains the audience, Jeremy changes

He has a nose for a lot of things, but I won't elaborate!

into a different set of clothing and a new vt record tape is laced up.

The second recording is usually as slickly organized as the first – and as successful with the studio audience! Jeremy is now triumphant. The production team are jubilant. The producer seems quite pleased but is fretting that some anticipated screamers only turned out to be woofers! Somebody shoves a drink into his hand and puts him into a corner. *FACING INWARDS!*

THE FINAL FURLONG

Five studio recordings yield ten programmes. Each programme has an *exact* duration, a programme number and a 'transmission spool number'.

The transmission order of the ten programmes is decided by Jeremy and the producer. As much thought goes into the transmission (tx order) as the running order for any show. Once the tx order is known the researchers phone all the stars to let them know the transmission date – they will obviously want to watch themselves! The transmission order is conveyed to LWT presentation, who are responsible for actually playing the correct tapes 'on the night'.

TV Times billings are written by the producer and programme associate and are passed to the LWT press officer along with VHS of all the shows for promotional purposes.

The series has been 'put to bed'. The production team has disbanded and all are enjoying holidays before starting on new programme assignments.

But the Tuesday following the first transmission letters begin to cascade into the LWT post room. The next series is beginning to take shape. The producer rolls his eyes heavenwards before opening the first of thousands of envelopes.

THE MOST REQUESTED REPEAT

The letters roll in for the next series – and requests for repeats. So far, 'The Great Frascati Fiddle' is in the lead. So here it is!

A letter was received from Mrs Gaynor Round of Basingstoke, Hants, who wanted to play a joke on a family friend, Tony Moroncini. An Italian, Tony had not lost his love of Italian wines in nearly twenty years of living in Britain – in fact, he bought special grapes to brew his own vintage. Could we think of anything? It was simple: Tony would be accused of running a winery and selling the juice in direct defiance of a Common Market edict. The scam required a government 'VAT official',

an official 'tester' (who mimed alcoholic paralysis as a result of drinking the stuff), and Jeremy as a police inspector who would 'test' Tony for tipsiness on arriving to investigate 'the disturbance'.

Tony arrived home with his wife, Alice, and Gwynn to find that his house had been turned into a bonded warehouse and all his wine and wine-making equipment was in the process of being confiscated. Tony immediately went 'bananas'. A strong Italian accent thickened by anger meant that the actor posing as the Vat man could barely understand a word of what was being said.

The scene is set: Tony's house has been turned into a bonded warehouse and all the paraphernalia of wine making is about to be confiscated.

Tony arrives home and wants to know what is going on.

Tony explodes.

Posing as a police inspector, Jeremy arrives to 'investigate the disturbance'.

The 'Vat man' explains to an incredulous Tony that he is in breech of Common Market law.

Suspected of being drunk, Tony is given a basic test for sobriety.

The reveal.

By this time Tony is beginning to suspect a wind-up.

BEADLE'S ABOUT

AND FINALLY A VERY TOUCHING STORY

The first scam to be shot in the 1988 series of *Beadle's About* was 'Jingle Shop'. In cahoots with an employment agency, temporary staff would be sent along to an 'office' – in fact, a sound recording studio. But a recording studio with a difference! This recording studio manufactured personalized answerphone jingles. No sooner had Phillip Howarth sat

down than he was being asked to 'help out' with a jingle for a client. But more complications were to arise. Coincidentally, all the studios' own reply jingles had been accidently 'wiped'. This meant that Phillip would be expected to sing the reply jingles live! Not only that! Each of the three incoming lines registered a different style of musical reply: opera, rock and ballad – and an instrumental 'finale' to be played by our punter!

Phillip battled his way through and became a star. But there was a particularly pleasant end to this story. Phillip had become separated from his brother Alan. Phillip was convinced that he was the sole survivor of the family. And so was Alan! As a result of watching *Beadle's About* Alan recognized Phillip and it was only a matter of time before they were reunited.

A ONE-MAN BAND!

HOW TO SET UP A BEADLE'S ABOUT SCAM

Write to the following address giving as much information as you are able regarding the person to set up and the basic plot. Write to:

Jeremy Beadle
London Weekend Television
London SE1 9LT

forget to put a stamp on the envelope! And don't